# Who Is Bono?

by Pam Pollack and Meg Belviso

illustrated by Andrew Thomson

Penguin Workshop

For Hiro Savage, who makes himself heard—PP

For C.O., a sun so bright it leaves no shadows
—MB

For Rhia—AT

PENGUIN WORKSHOP
An imprint of Penguin Random House LLC, New York

First published in the United States of America by Penguin Workshop,
an imprint of Penguin Random House LLC, New York, 2018



Visit us online at penguinrandomhouse.com.

Library of Congress Control Number: 2018036213

Printed in the United States of America

ISBN 9780448488684 (paperback) 10 9 8 7 6 5 4 3 2 WRZL
ISBN 9781524788513 (library binding) 10 9 8 7 6 5 4 3 2 1 WRZL

# Contents

Who Is Bono? . . . . . . . . . . . . . . . . . . . . . 1
Dublin . . . . . . . . . . . . . . . . . . . . . . . . . 4
Bono . . . . . . . . . . . . . . . . . . . . . . . . . 15
The Hype . . . . . . . . . . . . . . . . . . . . . . 24
Introducing U2 . . . . . . . . . . . . . . . . . . 34
New Beginnings . . . . . . . . . . . . . . . . . . 44
*War* . . . . . . . . . . . . . . . . . . . . . . . . . 49
Changing the World . . . . . . . . . . . . . . . 60
Different Directions . . . . . . . . . . . . . . . 74
A New Idea . . . . . . . . . . . . . . . . . . . . 85
A Voice for Everyone . . . . . . . . . . . . . . 95
Timelines . . . . . . . . . . . . . . . . . . . . 106
Bibliography . . . . . . . . . . . . . . . . . . 108

# Who Is Bono?

On March 2, 2007, the National Association for the Advancement of Colored People (NAACP)—an American organization that fights for civil rights and justice—presented a special award to a rock star. His name was Paul Hewson, but everyone called him Bono. He was being honored for the work he had done to raise money for the poor and sick, especially in Africa.

When Bono took the stage, he wore a dark suit and the oversize sunglasses he was famous for. His band, U2, was one of the most successful groups in music history. They played all over the world to sold-out stadium crowds. They'd won twenty-two Grammy Awards. Their records had sold millions of copies. They had fans everywhere they went.

But it didn't start out that way. Bono was born an ordinary boy in the Irish city of Dublin, where people who went to Catholic churches did not always get along with people who went to Protestant churches. Bono asked himself what God meant in a world where people suffered and wars were fought. He had taken all his questions and doubts and put them into song lyrics. When Bono took the stage, he didn't talk about rock and

roll. He talked about people who had nothing. People who were suffering. People who needed help. And he talked about one of the most important forces in his life: God. After all his years of questioning, Bono had learned one thing for sure: God wanted people to help one another.

"The poor are where God lives," Bono said. "God . . . is with the poor. And God is with us, if we are with them." Bono lived the kind of glamorous life he could only dream about as a boy. He had become a star. But once he had that life, he discovered there were more important things he needed to do. Not for himself, but for the world.

# CHAPTER 1
# Dublin

Paul David Hewson was born in Dublin, the capital city of Ireland, on May 10, 1960. His parents were Bob and Iris Hewson. He had one brother, Norman, who was seven years older. His father, Bob, worked for the post office.

Bob and Iris were both Christian, but they were different kinds of Christians. Bob was Catholic, and Iris was Protestant. In Dublin, it was very unusual for Catholics and Protestants to marry. The two groups did not get along. In Northern Ireland, fighting between Catholics and Protestants often became violent. Even as a young boy, Paul wondered why Christianity, which taught that people should love one another, made people hate one another.

## The Troubles

In the 1100s, England began to take control of the country of Ireland. They wanted to rule all the nations of the British Isles—England, Wales, Scotland, and Ireland. The Irish fought back. At that time both England and Ireland were Catholic countries. In the north, the fighting was particularly fierce. So England sent its own citizens to settle in Northern Ireland. Those people remained loyal to England. In the 1500s, the king declared the Church of England to be separate from the Catholic Church. Ireland was still a mostly Catholic country, except in the north, where so many descendants of English colonists lived.

In 1921, Northern Ireland officially became a separate country, and a part of the United Kingdom, which included England, Scotland, and Wales. But some people in Northern Ireland did not want to live under British rule. They started a group called the IRA (Irish Republican Army) that rebelled against the English. From 1968 to 1998, including during Bono's childhood, the conflict in Northern Ireland was called "the Troubles."

Paul did believe in fighting for *some* things. On his first day of school, a boy bit one of Paul's friends. Paul shoved the bully into a nearby railing!

When Paul got a Batman costume, he walked around his neighborhood telling everyone he was going to fight crime. Some older boys laughed at him. They pulled his Batman mask down over his eyes so he couldn't see anything.

The school that Paul went to was for Protestant children. He and his brother went to a Protestant church on Sundays with their mother while their Catholic father waited outside.

As Paul got older he started to think school was boring. Sometimes he didn't go at all. He just walked around the city of Dublin. His parents started to worry about his grades. When Paul was twelve, a new school opened near his house. It was called Mount Temple Comprehensive School.

It was different from other Dublin schools because it accepted all kids—Protestant and Catholic, boys and girls. The students at Mount Temple didn't wear uniforms, which was very unusual in Ireland. Paul's parents thought this new school might be a good place for him.

Paul liked Mount Temple. He got to wear different styles of clothes and became more confident. He made friends with other students, both boys and girls.

When he was twelve, Paul started playing chess with Norman and his father. He fell in love with the game. He wanted to play it all the time. When he heard about an international chess competition in Dublin, he entered even though he was only twelve. He was the youngest person in the whole tournament, so he stood out among all the other players. He liked the attention, even though he didn't win.

When he wasn't playing chess, Paul was often borrowing his brother's records. He liked a lot of popular performers, including David Bowie, the Beatles, and Led Zeppelin. He also liked Rory Gallagher, who happened to be Irish. There weren't many rock stars who were Irish.

Rory Gallagher

When Bono finally shopped for his very first record, he bought John Lennon and Yoko Ono's song "Happy Xmas (War is Over)." It was a Christmas song asking the world to end all wars.

## John Lennon (1940–1980)

John Lennon first became famous as a member of the Beatles—one of the most successful rock groups in history. He was a musician, singer, and songwriter. After the group split up, John Lennon recorded music on his own and with his wife, artist Yoko Ono.

John Lennon spoke out against war. He thought that people should learn to live in peace. One of his most famous songs, "Imagine," asks people to imagine a world without war. Tragically, in December 1980, John Lennon was killed in New York City. A memorial in Central Park was created in his honor.

Even though he didn't live in Northern Ireland, Paul was still very aware of the Troubles there. *That* war was very close to home.

On September 10, 1974, when Paul was fourteen years old, his mother died. She hadn't been sick, so it was a complete shock to everyone. Iris had collapsed at her own father's—Paul's grandfather's—funeral. Suddenly she was gone. Paul, his father, and his brother were left alone.

# CHAPTER 2
# Bono

Paul felt as if he had hardly gotten a chance to know his mother. He later said, "That house was no longer a home; it was just a house." Paul, Norman, and their father often argued with one another.

Since he didn't feel like he could talk to his father or brother, Paul thought he would try talking to God. He joined a prayer group at school. He hoped that praying would help him understand why his mother had been taken away from him.

There was a girl he liked in the grade behind him named Ali Stewart. She had dark brown hair and liked to wear gingham dresses and rubber boots. She didn't want to go out with Paul at first, but he hoped that she would one day change her mind.

Ali Stewart

In September 1976, when Paul was sixteen, he saw a note on the bulletin board at school. It had been put up by a younger boy named Larry Mullen. The note read: "Money wasted on a drum kit. Anyone done the same on guitars?" That was Larry's funny way of asking: Did anyone play guitar? Were they interested in starting a band with him?

Larry Mullen

Norman had played guitar a little and had given his younger brother an old acoustic guitar—a guitar that wasn't electric. Paul couldn't play it—he didn't even know how to tune it. But he liked the idea of being onstage. On September 25, 1976, Paul went over to Larry's house and said he would be the front man—the lead singer—of the new band. He didn't really know how to sing, either, but he didn't think that should matter. The rest of the band was Adam Clayton on bass and David Evans on guitar.

Adam Clayton David Evans

None of the band members were very experienced with their instruments. When they played, their amplifiers always screeched. This loud amplifier whistle was called feedback—so that's what the boys decided to call their band.

When Mount Temple announced a student talent show, Feedback signed up to perform. They played two songs that were popular that year: Peter Frampton's "Show Me the Way" and the Bay City Rollers' "Bye Bye Baby." How was their performance? One person who was in the audience said, "I just wanted it to end."

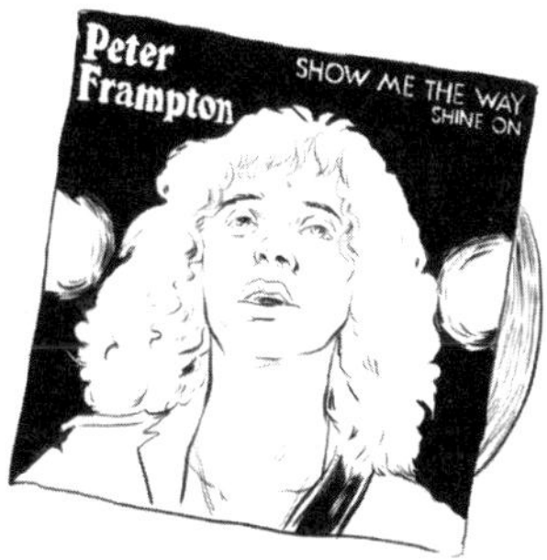


The band didn't play very well, but with Paul as their front man, they were still a hit. Paul loved being in front of a crowd. He walked around on the stage like a rock star and looked at the crowd as if he was really saying something important to them. Even though they missed a few notes and played a little sloppy, the performance made the band very popular at school.

Paul was thrilled. He devoted himself to studying other bands and singers. He also finally

got Ali Stewart to go out with him. He and his neighborhood friends created a club they called Lypton Village. They walked around the streets of Dublin and performed silly skits and jokes inspired by the British comedians called Monty Python.

Everyone in Lypton Village got a special nickname. David became known as “the Edge.” Paul was named Bono Vox after a store that sold hearing aids in Dublin. (He liked the name because it meant “good voice” in Latin.) The name was soon shortened to just Bono.

After a while, only his father called him Paul.

The Edge and Bono stuck with their Lypton Village nicknames for life.

## Monty Python

Monty Python sounds like one person, but it's actually a group of British performers: John Cleese, Eric Idle, Michael Palin, Graham Chapman, Terry Jones, and American illustrator Terry Gilliam. They became wildly popular through their TV show,

*Monty Python's Flying Circus*, which aired from 1969 to 1974. The Pythons were known for very silly comedy—the sillier the better. The group—who wrote and performed all their own material—went on to make successful funny movies as well, including *Monty Python and the Holy Grail.*

# CHAPTER 3
# The Hype

Feedback played songs written and made popular by other performers, like the Rolling Stones and Neil Young. In the late 1970s, Bono also went to see bands like the Ramones and the Clash perform live. Their music was loud, rude,

The Clash

and rough. But what Bono liked about them, especially the Clash, was that they sang about wanting to change the world. The Clash really wanted to *say* something with their music. Bono wanted to use music to make a statement, too.

Bono told the other guys in the band that instead of playing other people's songs, they should start writing their own. That way they could really put their own words—their own message—into the music. In 1977, they got a chance to play at another high school in Dublin called Saint Fintan's. For the first time, they'd be

paid to perform. Bono was sure they would be great. They'd been practicing a lot. They would play an American song from the 1950s called "Johnny B. Goode," and a more recent moody rock song, "Nights in White Satin." But when they started to play, Bono could see that the audience wasn't listening. Some people laughed. Bono realized he and the band had a lot more to learn about live performances.

When the show was over, Feedback was very embarrassed—but not ready to quit. Instead, they changed their name so no one would connect them to the terrible show at Saint Fintan's. They now called themselves the Hype.

Soon after, Bono was ready to graduate from Mount Temple. But he had failed Irish, the old language once spoken throughout Ireland. He had to return to school for another full year just to pass his Irish class. With only one class to take, he had plenty of time to think about writing

music. No one in the band had ever written a song before, but they had fun trying.

The band continued to practice. And Bono started to dream of becoming a rock star. But Bono cared about more than fame and money. He wanted to be a good person, too. He kept going to prayer meetings and reading the Bible. He tried hard to always follow the path that he thought God wanted for him. And he prayed that he would learn what that path might be.

In 1978, Adam saw an ad for a battle of the bands in Limerick, Ireland. The winner got a record demo with CBS Ireland and five hundred pounds, the equivalent of about $975 in the United States.

A demo is a professional recording made in a studio. It isn't meant to be sold. Copies of the demo are sent to record companies and producers so they can hear what a band or a singer sounds like. It was a rare opportunity for a band like Bono's to have the chance to record a real demo. If any of the record companies liked it, they would offer the band a recording contract—and that was the big-time!

Adam entered them in the contest, but he thought they should once again change their name. A friend had suggested the name U2. Bono liked the way it looked with only one letter and one number, and that it could also be read as "you too" or "you two." Most importantly, it was the cool name of an American spy plane.

The band—now known as U2—competed with musicians from all over Ireland. They didn't expect to do well—they just wanted the experience of being in the contest. They played three songs that they had written themselves. Writing their own original songs paid off. U2 ended up winning the contest! No one was more surprised than the band itself. Soon they were in a professional recording studio for the first time, getting ready to make their demo.

# The American U-2

After World War II, the biggest rivalry in the world was between two superpowers: the United States of America and the Soviet Union. The Soviet Union was made up of what is now Russia and other surrounding countries. The two superpowers didn't fight land battles. They spied on each other. And they worked hard to develop better and sneakier ways of spying.

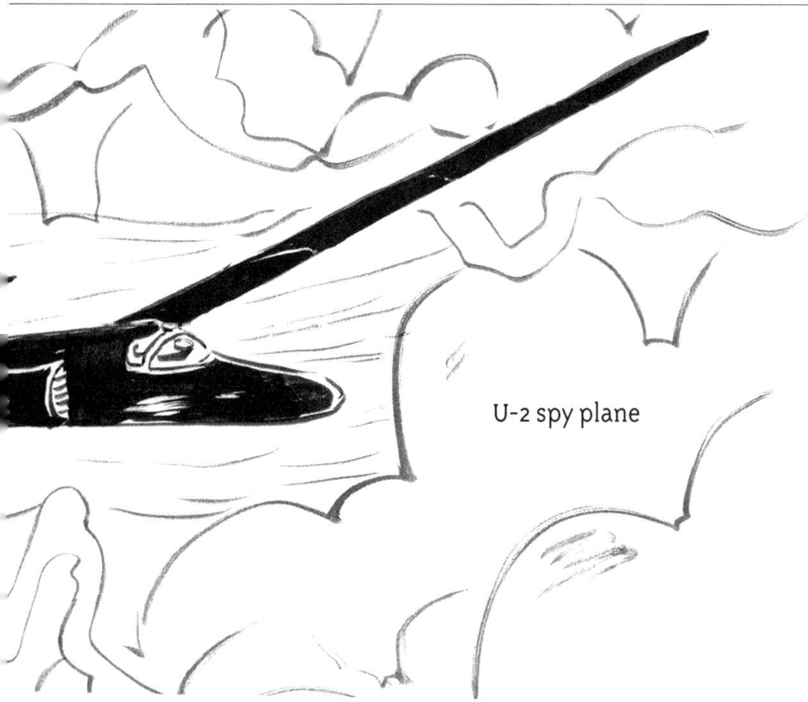

U-2 spy plane

In 1957, the United States developed a new kind of plane, the U-2. It could fly so high—up to seventy thousand feet—it couldn't be seen. The single-engine jet is nicknamed "Dragon Lady." And the current model, the U-2S, is still in service today for NASA, the US Air Force, and the CIA.

# CHAPTER 4
# Introducing U2

In the studio, the band made a tape with the three songs they'd written and performed in the contest: "Street Missions," "Life on a Distant Planet," and "The TV Song." These songs were about their own lives as young men in Dublin. In "Street Missions," they sang about walking around their town, looking at other people, and wondering what their lives were like.

The demo didn't get them a record contract but it did get the attention of a manager named Paul McGuinness. Paul wanted to help guide

Paul McGuinness

their career. U2 continued to play in clubs all over Ireland and the United Kingdom. They were getting more experience performing in front of a crowd. And sometimes, the audiences were not kind. The guys even had to defend themselves against people booing them onstage. Paul

McGuinness introduced the band to experienced musicians who could work with them and teach them more about performing. And he worked to get them more publicity.

One night, in a Dublin McDonald's, Bono and some friends from Lypton Village met a group of people who called themselves Shalom. Shalom was a group of people who prayed together, sort of like the prayer group Bono went to at school. They were not connected with any one church. They believed in talking to God themselves, rather than going to church. This really appealed to Bono. Soon he, the Edge, and Larry were going to prayer meetings with Shalom. Only Adam didn't join the group.

In April 1979, Bono and Ali went to London. They visited all the record companies they knew of and left them copies of U2's demo tape. Most weren't interested. But someone from CBS liked them. He came to see the band play in Dublin

and offered them a contract with CBS's Ireland division. It wasn't an international contract, but it was a start!

The band recorded one song for CBS called "11 O'Clock Tick Tock." The title came from a note left by one of his bandmates on the door when Bono missed a practice that was scheduled for eleven o'clock. CBS made only a thousand copies of the record, but they sold out immediately. U2 went right to work on their first real album. It was called *Boy* and it was produced by Steve Lillywhite, who had worked with a lot of famous artists. Bono loved how creative Steve was. He was always looking for interesting sounds. Steve broke bottles, tapped spoons on bicycle spokes, and even had Larry play his drums under the stairs to get a different sound.

Steve Lillywhite

The Edge, too, was experimenting. He ran his guitar through two different speakers to give it a distinct echoing sound.

Bono sang about the innocence of childhood and his fears of losing the sense of wonder that small children have. He made up his lyrics as he stood at the microphone.

*Boy* wasn't a huge hit even though the band traveled around the world performing and promoting it. One song on the album, "I Will Follow," was special for Bono. It was about the love a mother has for her son. Bono wrote the song with his own mother in mind.

On December 6, 1980, U2 played their first show in the United States at a rock club called the Ritz in New York City. The band felt a connection to America because so many Irish people had left Ireland to live there. Still, most of the people in the club that night had never heard of U2. They weren't interested in their music. But Bono got their attention. He climbed speakers and swung from the ceiling. After each song, more people gathered around the stage to hear Bono sing and the Edge play his guitar. By the end of the show, everyone was singing along.

When the band returned to Ireland, they were excited to start work on a new album called *October*. Bono, the Edge, and Larry were spending more time with the Shalom group. Adam felt left out. He worried that they didn't want him in the band anymore. When members of Shalom came to the studio, all work would stop so that they could pray together. Most of the songs on *October* were about God.

Some of the Shalom members told Bono, the Edge, and Larry that they didn't think God liked rock and roll. Larry quickly stopped going to Shalom meetings, but Bono and the Edge were confused. Did they have to choose between God and U2?

# CHAPTER 5
# New Beginnings

Bono's faith and his relationship with God had always been very important to him. When he was onstage playing to an audience, he felt closest to God. Music was his way of sharing his faith. In the song "Gloria," he sang, "Oh Lord, if I had anything, anything at all, I'd give it to you." The song was a prayer asking God to sing through him.

But why did some religious people—like the Shalom prayer group—think that rock and roll couldn't exist alongside a true love of God? Music was like prayer to the Edge as well. It seemed so wrong to both him and Bono that they should have to make such a choice.

Eventually, both Bono and the Edge chose U2. Bono stayed friends with many of the people in Shalom, but he had to follow his own heart.

The new album, *October*, was released in October 1981. U2 went back on tour in Europe and the United States to promote it. At that time, something new and exciting was emerging within the music industry: the cable television channel called MTV.

U2's video for the song "Gloria" was one of the earliest videos to be played on the new station. People in the United States were starting to get to know U2.

## MTV (Music Television)

MTV started broadcasting on August 1, 1981. The channel played music videos twenty-four hours a day with breaks only for commercials and news. Its target audience was teenagers and young adults.

MTV quickly became an important force in music, first in the United States and then worldwide. A popular video could make a band, a singer, or a song famous overnight. Very quickly, the fashion industry, movies, and other television networks all looked to MTV and music videos for inspiration, trends, and hot topics.

On August 21, 1982, Bono and Ali got married just outside of Dublin. Bono had asked Adam to be his best man. At the wedding reception, Bono's older brother, Norman, put him on his shoulders and carried him around the room while everyone, including Bono's father, cheered. Bono and Ali had been dating for five years. She knew what it would be like having a husband in a rock band who was often on tour. She was busy studying political science at University College Dublin.

Bono and Ali traveled to Jamaica for their honeymoon. When they returned home, Ali went back to school and Bono went back on tour with the band.

## CHAPTER 6
## *War*

There were many things that Bono loved about America. But when he traveled to the United States, people often wanted to talk about the Troubles in Northern Ireland. Many American U2 fans were the descendants of Irish Catholic immigrants. Those immigrants held on to their anger toward England when they moved to the United States. It seemed that many Americans supported the IRA. They wanted *all* of Ireland to be independent, and they expected U2, as an Irish band, to agree with them. Sometimes fans even threw money onstage as the band played. They hoped U2 would donate it in support of the IRA.

Bono hadn't grown up in Northern Ireland,

but he knew this fight had caused a lot of suffering. He thought there was something very wrong about fans wanting to donate money to pay for bombs that might kill people in the streets. He didn't think they really understood what war was like.

Bomb explosion in Northern Ireland

In March 1982, U2 was asked to be in the Saint Patrick's Day parade in New York City. The band agreed. But when they discovered that the parade was being dedicated to an important IRA leader, they decided not to participate.

As citizens of Ireland, U2 was always asked to take a stand on the Troubles. For Bono and the rest of the band, their stand was that they thought the fighting should end. They didn't want to support hurting people in any way.

When he got back to Ireland, Bono couldn't stop thinking about all the violence going on in the world. The band decided to call their new album *War*. The song "New Year's Day" was about political protests in Poland. "Seconds" was about the threat of nuclear weapons. The album's most famous song was called "Sunday Bloody Sunday."

The message of U2's "Sunday Bloody Sunday" was not for or against the IRA. It was simply a call to end all the fighting. Bono sang, "I *won't* heed the battle call." He sang about "broken bottles under children's feet" and "bodies strewn across the dead-end street." The song was angry but it was against more violence.

The album *War* was released in February 1983. It quickly went right to number one in the United Kingdom. Crowds especially loved the song "Sunday Bloody Sunday." While on tour, a photographer named Anton Corbijn took black-and-white photos of the group in the snow in Sweden. In the age of MTV, what a band looked like was sometimes as important as their music. And Anton's photos showed U2 looking tough and rugged.

Anton Corbijn

They looked like they would not back down from a fight.

When the tour got to Ireland, Bono was nervous about playing the song in his home country. Would people be angry at the message?

## Bloody Sunday

On Sunday, January 30, 1972, thirteen people in Derry, Northern Ireland, were killed by British police and another thirteen were injured. The police had been breaking up a local protest against British rule. Some protestors threw stones at the police, who chased and shot them.

People were shocked that the police had shot at unarmed people. They called it "Bloody Sunday." Not all Irish people agreed on the question of British rule, but everyone was stunned by what happened to the twenty-six protestors and never forgot it.

The first city in Northern Ireland where U2 played the song was Belfast—a city at the very center of the Troubles. Bono said to the crowd there, "This is not a rebel song. We're gonna play it for you here in Belfast. If you don't like it, you let us know."

The crowd in Belfast did let him know—they loved the song. They saw the violence all around them. And the people of Belfast agreed with Bono. They were tired of war in their streets.

Bono felt like he was finally using his music to say something important. He was more proud of *War* than anything he had ever done. The words he had written, set to the music the band created together, had started to make people think about the terrible effects of war.

# CHAPTER 7
## Changing the World

U2 was still very interested in talking about the problems of the world. But for their next album, they did not want to sound exactly the way they had on *War*. *The Unforgettable Fire* was a more artistic record than the straightforward rock and roll of their last album.

On the new album, Bono wrote a song dedicated to Martin Luther King Jr. He admired how King not only fought for civil rights but did it without the use of violence. Bono wrote the song "Pride

Martin Luther King Jr.

(In the Name of Love)" in honor of Dr. King.

In "Pride," Bono sang:

*Early morning, April four,*
*Shot rings out in the Memphis sky.*
*Free at last, they took your life*
*They could not take your pride.*

Bono was not the only singer who saw music as a way to change the world. Bob Geldof was a member of another Irish band called the Boomtown Rats. Bob was upset by a terrible drought in the African nation of Ethiopia. A lack of water was killing the crops that people needed to survive. And a civil war at the time made it even harder for Ethiopians to get help. Bob asked his friends in the music industry to join him and record a new song. All the profits earned from the song would go to the starving people in Ethiopia.

Bob Geldof

## Martin Luther King Jr. (1929–1968)

Martin Luther King Jr. was born in Atlanta, Georgia. He grew up to be a Baptist minister and leader of the African American civil rights movement. His nonviolent protests were based on his Christian beliefs. He helped organize the 1963 March on Washington, where he delivered his famous "I Have a Dream" speech.

In 1964, he won the Nobel Peace Prize for his work in advancing African American civil rights through nonviolent protest. He was assassinated on April 4, 1968, in Memphis, Tennessee.

Bono eagerly accepted the invitation to join other singers from Ireland and the United Kingdom to record the song called "Do They Know It's Christmas?" Adam went along with him. The song was recorded in November 1984. It was the number-one song in the United Kingdom by Christmas. Bob Geldof planned a benefit concert with performers from all over the world. The benefit was called Live Aid.

## Live Aid (July 13, 1985)

Live Aid was a concert held at Wembley Stadium in London and the John F. Kennedy Stadium in Philadelphia on the same day. Many of the biggest stars of the time performed throughout the day, including Queen, Sting, Phil Collins, David Bowie, Duran Duran, and Madonna. Inspired by the idea,

other cities held their own benefit concerts on the same day in countries like West Germany, Australia, Japan, and the Soviet Union.

Live Aid had an estimated audience of 1.9 billion people watching around the world. The benefit raised $125 million for the starving people of Ethiopia.

U2 thought "Pride" was the perfect song to play at Live Aid. During the concert, Bono stopped singing to dance with a girl in the audience. Bono had done this before, but now the band was under a strict time limit. And by the time he'd finished dancing with the girl, that limit was up. The rest of the band was furious. They hadn't even played the song!

Bono felt terrible. He hoped that he hadn't ruined Live Aid for the rest of the band. But it turned out the audience loved it. Seeing Bono dancing with a member of the audience made the entire crowd feel like he was connecting with them personally. U2 became more popular than ever.

After Live Aid, Bono and Ali went to Ethiopia themselves for five weeks. They wanted to meet the people they were trying to help.

They also wanted to spend time together. Because the band toured so often, Bono and Ali were often separated. Bono's feelings about his wife inspired him to write the song "With or Without You." He sang to Ali:

*Through the storm we reach the shore*
*You gave it all, but I want more.*

Along with "With or Without You," U2's next album, *The Joshua Tree*, included "Where the Streets Have No Name," which was about Bono's experiences in Ethiopia, and "I Still Haven't Found What I'm Looking For." In that song, Bono showed that after all this time, he was still devoted to God. He sang, "I have scaled these city walls . . . only to be with you."

But he still wasn't sure he was doing what God wanted. Was playing music enough? Throughout the 1980s, U2 played many concerts that brought awareness to injustices around the world. They played for Amnesty International, a group that fought for people who were wrongly put in jail.

They played a concert against apartheid, a system where black South Africans were mistreated and not given the same rights as white South Africans. And the concert profits were donated to the people who needed the money the most.

*The Joshua Tree* was U2's most popular album yet. It was inspired by the time the band had spent in America. Bono had started listening to gospel and folk music as well as American blues artists like B. B. King and Muddy Waters. He'd met and become friends with the American music legend Bob Dylan, who encouraged him to study the roots of rock and roll.

Bono and the band put all these experiences into the songs on the new album. It topped the charts in over twenty countries, including the United States. In April 1987, U2 was on the cover of *TIME* magazine, which said theirs was the concert everyone wanted to see.

Bono was changing people's ideas of what a rock star was. Instead of being known for living a glamorous, irresponsible life, he was trying to make the world a better place.

# CHAPTER 8
# Different Directions

By 1989, Bono and Ali had been married for almost seven years. On May 10, 1989, they had their first child, a daughter named Jordan. Bono was twenty-nine years old. He was one of the most popular rock stars in the world. He wanted to use his fame to inspire people.

But in some ways, being famous made it more difficult to connect personally with fans. When U2 was an unknown band singing about war and poverty, people believed them. Now that they were playing giant arenas and were on the covers of magazines, people wondered if the band really cared about things like that. After all, their lives were so different from the lives of ordinary people. Maybe they just thought it was cool to talk about these things so they could sell more albums and more tickets.

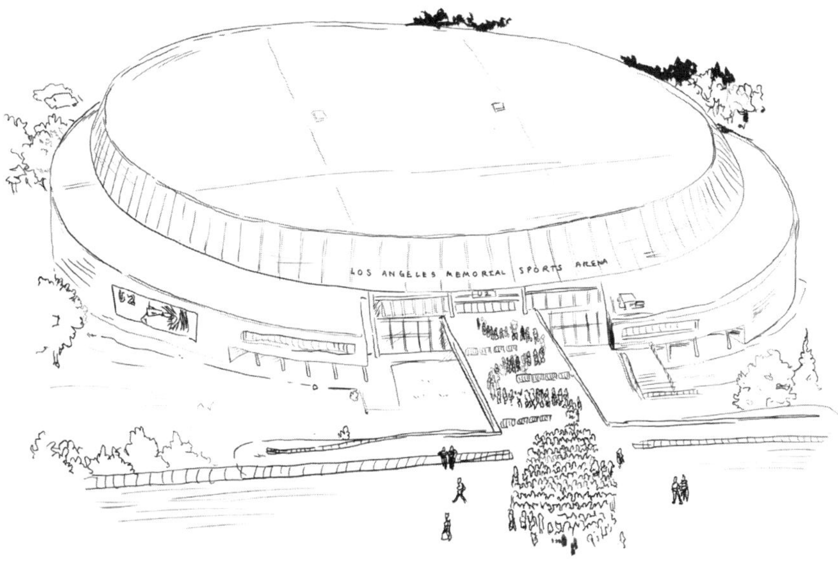

Bono told the band they had to "go away and dream it all up again." He wanted U2 to remember the things they truly believed in. He thought they needed a change. And, in 1989, one of the biggest symbols of the Cold War—the Berlin Wall—was about to come down. This was a huge signal that the world was changing, too.

On November 9, 1989, citizens of Berlin started attacking the wall from both sides with axes and picks. The time for division was over. It was the first step toward all of Germany coming together as one country again. Bono was thrilled to see it happen. He and the band flew to Berlin on October 3, 1990, the same day Germany was officially reunited.

## The Berlin Wall

When Germany was defeated in World War II, the country was divided into four sections. Each section was controlled by one of the countries on the winning side: the United States, the United Kingdom, France, and the Soviet Union. The capital city of Berlin was in the Soviet section, but it, too, was divided into four sections.

As the relationship between the Soviet Union and the rest of the world grew chillier—a time that was known as the Cold War—it became more difficult to travel between East Germany and West Germany. In the city of Berlin, an actual wall had been built in 1961 to cut off West Berlin from the rest of the city. The wall became a symbol of the Cold War and the fight between Communist countries in the East and more democratic nations of the West.

Everyone in Berlin was excited about the future. And so was Bono. He had a lot of ideas for new songs. The band decided to stay in Berlin to record an album.

Back home in Ireland, Bono and Ali had another daughter, Memphis Eve. She was born June 7, 1991.

Ali and the girls didn't come with Bono on tour. So the family didn't see one another for weeks at a time. It was hard for the girls when Bono went away. When he was at home, they wanted their father to stay, but Bono and the band usually had more shows to perform.

The band's new album was called *Achtung Baby*. (*Achtung* is German for "attention" or "watch out!") The members of U2 were now truly international superstars. Throughout the nineties, their music moved beyond the world of rock

and roll. They began to write songs for movies like *Batman Forever* and the James Bond movie *GoldenEye*. Bono even sang on an album called *Duets* with one of the most famous singers in the world, Frank Sinatra. Bono was a big fan. He loved the way Frank Sinatra sang. But he never thought he'd get a chance to sing with Sinatra himself. It was a dream come true for Bono.

## Francis Albert “Frank” Sinatra (1915–1998)

Frank Sinatra, also known as “Old Blue Eyes,” was one of the first singers to have a huge teenage following. In the years before rock and roll, his fans, called “bobby-soxers” after their short white socks, jumped and screamed when he was onstage. He went on to become one of the best-selling singers of all time. His fifty-year career included success as an actor and producer as well.

Frank Sinatra was awarded the Grammy Legend Award as well as the Grammy Lifetime Achievement Award.

Maybe one of the most satisfying things to happen for Bono in the 1990s was in 1998, when the two sides in the Irish conflict took steps to end the violence. Representatives from both sides of the fight sat down to sign an agreement. It stated that most people in Northern Ireland wanted to remain part of the United Kingdom and most people in the Republic of Ireland—along with some people in Northern Ireland—wished to be independent from the United Kingdom. Both sides agreed to try to resolve their differences in a peaceful and democratic way. Although the agreement didn't stop the fighting completely, it was an important step in the right direction.

British prime minister Tony Blair and Irish leader Bertie Ahern

In February 1999, Bono was rushed to the hospital with shortness of breath. Years of singing loudly onstage had taken a toll on Bono's voice. The doctors warned him that his throat was very damaged. But Bono couldn't imagine taking a break from singing. Even if his voice was damaged, he thought what he had to say was important.

On August 17, 1999, Ali and Bono had their first son, Elijah Bob Patricius Guggi Q.

The twentieth century was almost over. But Bono had plenty of ideas for the twenty-first.

# CHAPTER 9
# A New Idea

By 2000, Bono had traveled all over the world. He had seen that people in some countries were much poorer than those in more developed nations. Some countries owed a lot of money to wealthy governments around the globe. Out of the forty-one countries that had the most debt, thirty-three of them were in Africa! Bono thought it was wrong that people didn't have enough money to build hospitals or schools because their countries owed so much money. Especially since some of the richer countries had made a lot of money exporting the natural resources of these poor countries without giving the people anything in return.

Bono thought that the beginning of a new century was the perfect time to "free" the poor of the world from debt. He wanted wealthy countries to forgive the debt of poorer nations. He saw this as the only way for the poor to recover.

He started traveling the world, talking to government leaders. Now, instead of standing onstage and talking to a crowd, Bono was talking to presidents, prime ministers, and congresspeople. He even met with Pope John Paul II. He wrote letters and scheduled private meetings. He made speeches.

Many politicians were surprised at how much Bono knew about the world. They thought he wouldn't really understand what the debt meant to poor countries. But they were wrong. Bono did his homework and he truly believed in what he was saying. He thought it was the right thing to do. Bono was becoming known as a humanitarian, a person who works to make other people's lives better.

In between talking to world leaders, Bono flew back to Dublin as often as he could. His father was very sick with cancer, and Bono spent long hours with him in his hospital room. Then he'd visit with his brother, Norman, who owned a successful restaurant in the city.

Norman's restaurant, Tosca

And U2 continued to record and grow in popularity. In 2000, the Grammy Awards named the single "Beautiful Day" song of the year. In

2001, the group won the Grammy Award for best rock performance by a group, and their album *All That You Can't Leave Behind* won a Grammy for best rock album. Just a few months later, Bono and Ali had their fourth child, John Abraham. The baby was only three months old when Bono's father died. The night his father died, Bono dedicated the concert he was playing to his father. He said, "I want to thank my old man, my father, for giving me this voice."

A few weeks later, on September 11, 2001, terrorists attacked the World Trade Center in New York City and the Pentagon building outside Washington, DC, using airplanes as weapons. U2 participated in a tribute concert called America: A Tribute to Heroes. It was held to benefit victims, their families, New York City firefighters, and

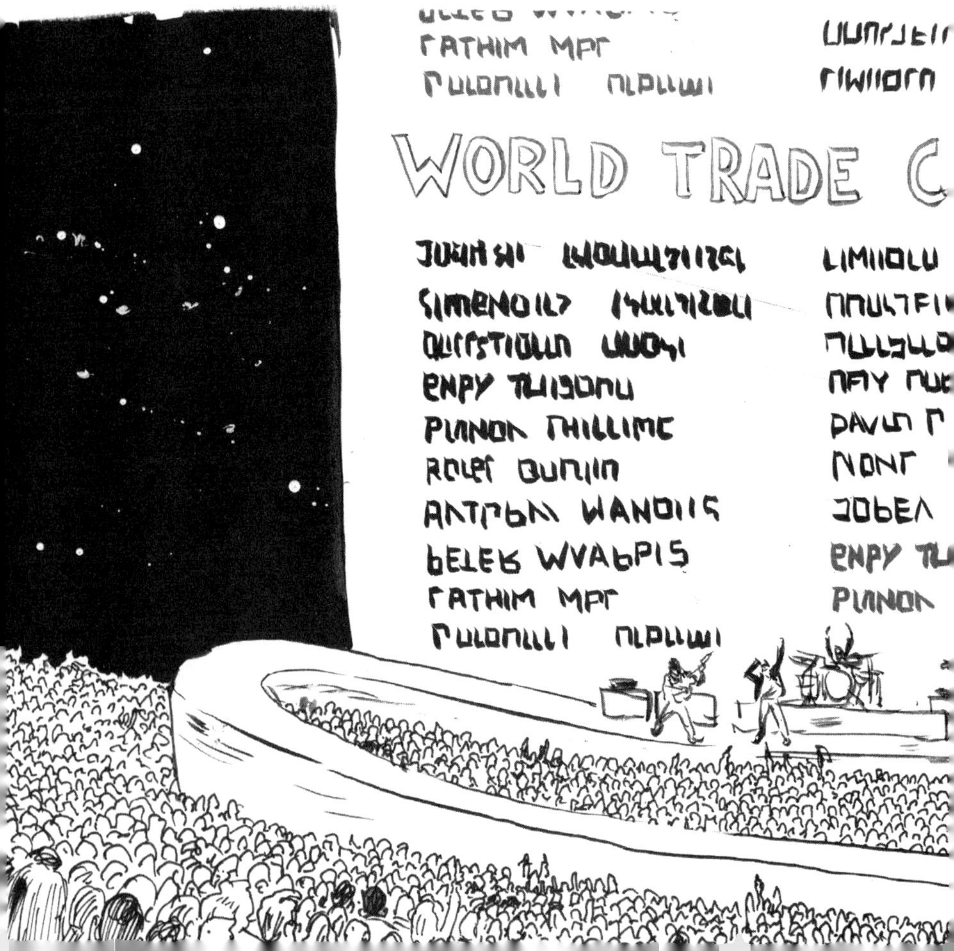

NYC police officers. A few months later, when U2 performed at the Super Bowl Halftime Show, they dedicated their performance to the victims of 9/11. As Bono sang, the names of the thousands of people who died in the attack scrolled on the wall behind him.

Bono's humanitarian efforts continued. He helped establish a brand name called PRODUCT (RED) to raise money to fight diseases like AIDS, tuberculosis, and malaria. PRODUCT (RED) partnered with huge corporations like Apple, Gap, Nike, Coca-Cola, and Penguin Classics to raise awareness and money.

He and Ali started a company called EDUN for clothing made in Africa. They hoped this would make other people want to work with

developing African countries. The problems of poverty were not going to be solved overnight, but Bono liked knowing he was helping to find solutions. He was willing to work hard to promote trade in Africa.

In October 2002, the Irish government created a stamp that featured U2. It was part of their Irish Rock Legends stamps that also included Rory Gallagher, one of Bono's earliest inspirations.

In December 2005, Bono, along with Bill Gates, the founder of Microsoft Corporation, and his wife, Melinda Gates, was named Person of the Year by *TIME* magazine. He'd been a rock star for over twenty years. Now Bono was internationally famous for his work for the common good of people all over the world.

## CHAPTER 10
## A Voice for Everyone

By 2005, music was changing. When U2 started out, people bought vinyl records and cassette tapes. Now music was digital, stored in computer memory. Bono saw this was the way of the future. He made a deal with Steve Jobs, the cofounder of Apple, to sell all of U2's music in the digital music store called iTunes. At that time, if you opened up iTunes on your computer, the section marked "Artists" showed the shadow of a man singing at a microphone. That was the iTunes symbol for all the recording artists you could find on iTunes. It was also a picture of Bono.

## Steve Jobs (1955–2011)

Steve Jobs grew up in California and was fascinated by machines.

On April 1, 1976, Steve, who was just twenty-one years old, and his friend Steve Wozniak, started a company they called Apple Computer in Steve's parents' garage. Under Steve's leadership, Apple would go on to become the most successful computer company in the world, introducing such products as the Macintosh computer, the iMac, the MacBook, the iPod, the iPhone, and the iPad.

Steve Jobs had decided to let Bono represent a part of the iTunes brand when they'd first started working together.

In 2005, U2 came to the United States to perform at a concert to raise money for the victims of Hurricane Katrina. Lake Pontchartrain had flooded the streets of New Orleans. Homes were destroyed. People were stranded for days waiting for someone to rescue them. Bono sang the song "One":

> *One life with each other: sisters, brothers . . .*
> *We get to carry each other . . .*

The lyrics were meant to rally people to stand together and to help one another.

In 2007, Bono got a very surprising honor. He was knighted in recognition of his service and his humanitarian work.

In 2009, when Barack Obama was sworn in as president, U2 performed at his inauguration. The concert took place on the same steps where

Dr. Martin Luther King Jr. gave his "I Have a Dream" speech. U2 performed "Pride (In the Name of Love)," dedicated to Dr. King.

Bono was getting used to talking to the most powerful people in the world. He wanted to speak for poor people everywhere who would never get the chance to meet with a president or a queen. When the NAACP gave him a special award for his humanitarian work, he said, "God, my friends, is with the poor. And God is with us, if we are with them."

Bono and the Edge now had their eye on a different stage. They wrote the music for a Broadway musical called *Spider-Man: Turn Off the Dark*. The show was based on Marvel Comics' Spider-Man character. It featured a lot of complicated stunts. The actors sometimes flew around the stage on ropes and "webs" and performed fight scenes. Unfortunately, the stunts were dangerous and several actors were hurt. *Spider-Man: Turn Off the Dark* was the most expensive Broadway production in history!

*Spider-Man* was performed in New York

City, so Bono and Ali moved there with their sons to work on it. Their daughters, Jordan and Eve, already lived in New York. Jordan went to Columbia University and Eve went to New York University. Bono and Ali missed the girls so much, they were happy to be in the city with them. After the show was over, the whole family stayed in New York.

*Spider-Man* ended in 2014. By then, Jordan and Eve were twenty-five and twenty-three years old. Their brothers were now fifteen and thirteen. One day that year, Bono was riding his bike in Central Park when he swerved to keep from hitting someone else. He fell down. He was seriously injured, especially on his face, arm, and hand. But a few months later, Bono appeared on TV to show everyone he was okay.

Bono enjoyed his life with his family in New York. But he still traveled around the world with U2. On November 14 and 15, 2015, the band

Bono and U2 on *The Tonight Show* with Jimmy Fallon

was scheduled to play in Paris, France. But the shows were canceled when there was a terrorist attack. Some of the people who lost their lives had been at a rock concert.

Bono wrote a special song as a tribute to the city, which he and the band performed a few weeks later at a special concert. The song was a celebration of the city's spirit, which would never be broken.

As always, he wanted to give a voice to people who couldn't be heard. When Bono first dreamed of being a rock star, he imagined himself as the center of attention. But when he reached center stage, he saw a world full of people who needed attention more than he did.

And that is Bono's legacy: He continues to be the rock star who wants to shine brighter. For Bono, "Music can change the world because it can change people."

# Timeline of Bono's Life

| | |
|---|---|
| 1960 | Paul David "Bono" Hewson is born on May 10 |
| 1976 | The future U2 band members meet for their first rehearsal |
| 1978 | U2 wins a contest to record their demo tape |
| 1979 | U2 signs their first contract with CBS Ireland |
| 1980 | U2's first single, "11 O'Clock Tick Tock," is released |
| | U2's first album, *Boy*, is released |
| 1982 | Marries Ali Stewart |
| 1983 | U2's third album, *War*, is released |
| 1985 | U2 performs at Live Aid |
| 1987 | *The Joshua Tree* album is released |
| 1989 | Jordan Hewson is born |
| 1991 | Memphis Eve Sunny Day Hewson is born |
| 1999 | Elijah Bob Patricius Guggi Q Hewson is born |
| | Meets with Pope John Paul II in Italy |
| 2001 | John Abraham Hewson is born |
| 2005 | Named one of *TIME* magazine's Persons of the Year |
| 2006 | PRODUCT (RED) is founded |
| 2007 | Named a Knight of the British Empire |
| 2011 | *Spider-Man: Turn Off the Dark* opens on Broadway |

## Timeline of the World

| | |
|---|---|
| 1960 | Domino's Pizza is founded |
| 1963 | Dr. Seuss's book *Hop on Pop* is published |
| 1968 | Martin Luther King Jr. is assassinated |
| 1971 | Apollo 15 lands on the moon |
| 1972 | Bob Douglas becomes the first African American elected to the Basketball Hall of Fame |
| 1977 | First killer whale is born in captivity in California |
| 1979 | The Sahara Desert experiences snow for thirty minutes |
| 1981 | First London Marathon begins with 7,500 runners |
| 1986 | Pixar Animation Studios opens in California |
| 1996 | First Pokémon video game is released in Japan |
| 2004 | Facebook launches |
| 2005 | Hurricane Katrina devastates the US Gulf Coast, killing nearly two thousand people |
| 2006 | Scientists vote that Pluto is too small to be a planet. It is named a dwarf planet |
| 2015 | Ireland becomes the first country to make same-sex marriage legal by popular vote |
| 2017 | Donald Trump is sworn in as the forty-fifth president of the United States |

# Bibliography


***Books for young readers**

Assayas, Michka. ***Bono on Bono: Conversations with Michka Assayas.*** New York: Riverhead Books, 2005.

Brankin, Una. "Norman Hewson—Dining Out With World Celebrities." ***Sunday Mirror***, January 23, 2000, www.atu2.com/news/norman-hewson-dining-out-with-world-celebrities.html.

Carr, David. "Chasing Relevancy at Any Cost, Even Free." ***New York Times***, November 10, 2014.

Coscarelli, Joe. "Heading Back to Paris, Defiantly." ***New York Times***, December 6, 2015.

Chatterton, Mark. ***U2: The Complete Encyclopedia.*** London: Firefly Publishing, 2001.

Jobling, John. ***U2: The Definitive Biography.*** New York: Thomas Dunne Books, 2014.

*Kootnikoff, David. ***Bono: A Biography.*** Santa Barbara, CA: Greenwood Press, 2012.

U2. ***U2: Guitar Chord Songbook.*** Milwaukee: Hal Leonard Corporation, 1988.

**Websites**

www.u2.com